£1.50

13

CREATIVE WOOD SCULPTURE

from natural form

The author fashioning an abstract sculpture from natural form.

CREATIVE WOOD SCULPTURE

from natural form

Graeme Bentham

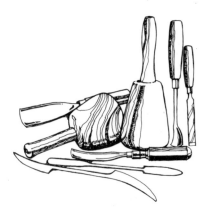

BLANDFORD PRESS

POOLE   DORSET

First published 1978
Copyright © 1978 Blandford Press Ltd.
Link House, West Street
Poole, Dorset BH15 1LL

ISBN 0 7137 0874 3

Filmset in 'Monophoto' Baskerville 12 on 13 pt. by
Richard Clay (The Chaucer Press), Ltd., Bungay, Suffolk
and printed in Great Britain by Fletcher & Son Ltd., Norwich
Colour plates printed by Woodwards Ltd., Bath

Contents

Acknowledgements

All of the carvings, sculptures and photographs are the work of the author.

The line illustrations were prepared by David Dowland from the author's sketches and from the catalogues of Alec Tiranti Ltd, with kind permission.

Sculpture in wood has a history almost as long as that of the human race. This is the famous wooden statue of King Setti I (1300 B.C.) from the Royal Room, Valley of the Kings, near Thebes in ancient Egypt.

Introduction

For about 3 million years the human race and trees have grown and lived together, sharing a mutually dependent existence.

Trees and shrubs are beautiful to look at and help satisfy some deep felt need, but they are also essential to our existence and healthy functioning.

It is not surprising that throughout the ages people have instinctively cared for trees and used the timber, not only for utilitarian purposes, but also for its sacred, artistic and pleasurable qualities.

Today, more than ever, in an atmosphere of ever increasing technological advances, pressured industry and recreation, people are once again turning to the stabilising influences of Nature to experience the more durable and satisfying activities. This is especially apparent in the renewed interest and growth of the time honoured skills and crafts which tend to lead to closer contact and harmonious association with the natural environment.

Trees are to be found almost everywhere in the world. Where they are scarce, they are considered precious. Thus, it is not surprising that the shaping and carving of wood is one of the oldest of human activities.

Both as craft and as an artistic medium, the fashioning of wood is a thoughtful process requiring individual skill, patience, perseverance and imagination, if the accomplishment of personal creative experience is to be achieved.

For fulfilment this need not be difficult, elaborate or laborious. The best results are more often attained by the simplest of means and recognition of happy accidents.

To
Jill Rosemary Bentham

Basic Equipment

For the serious sculptor, a good strong bench is essential, and a strong table, preferably reinforced, should serve quite well for the amateur or beginner.

A good bench can easily be made, improvised or bought, according to your pocket. The size and type will depend upon the nature of the work involved.

The bench should provide a good solid support with minimum of bounce. This is important considering the heavy banging it will have to carry. The height should be slightly higher than that of the normal carpenter's bench, and should have a projecting edge so that G-clamps may be used.

The top should be thick enough to support a carver's vice and have a hole ($\frac{3}{4}$ in) bored at intervals so that the easily-movable wooden vice, carver's bench screws and various clamps can be fitted.

A solid, four-legged, kitchen or dining-room table can easily be converted and strengthened where necessary.

To prevent bounce, the bench can be secured to the floor or wall; but if the table weight is sufficient, it is an advantage to have mobility.

Securing Work to Bench

The method used should depend upon the type of job and available resources.

A most satisfactory method of securing flat boards is the use of a G-clamp which can be bought in various sizes; one of 8–10 in will cover a wide range of work.

Occasionally, a joiner's sash-clamp may come in useful.

A garden shed converted to make an adequate studio for wood sculpture.

Method of securing timber to side of bench using G-clamp.

A G-clamp used for securing fairly large flat surfaces.

Where it is necessary to turn the model and work all around, a carver's bench screw is very useful. These can be bought in a range of sizes, from 4 to 12 in, the choice depending upon the size of the work. When in use, a hard wood block, roughly 3 in square, is used as a washer on the underside of the bench. This saves time in screwing up. If the work height needs increasing, a second block may be placed under the model. The butterfly nut should be tight in order to keep the work firmly in position.

Where a vice is needed, the wooden carver's vice or chops is ideal. This type of vice is fitted on top of the bench by passing a strong screw through a hole bored through the bench top and secured by a large butterfly nut from underneath.

Holes bored at intervals allow the vice to be moved readily and may also be used for bench screws.

Bench screw and butterfly nut. Various shaped beech blocks are used as washers and for raising the height of the model where necessary. A hole is bored through the bench.

The method of securing a small carving using bench screw and butterfly nut.

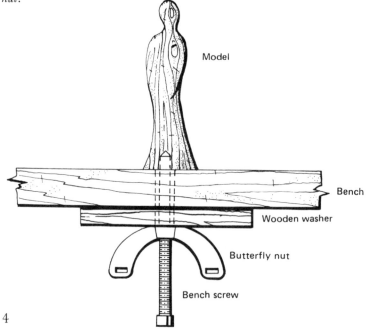

Model

Bench

Wooden washer

Butterfly nut

Bench screw

The carver's vice is quite strong and capable of holding a model of good size and weight. Being on top of the bench, it stands up well to heavy work and can be used for quite long pieces of work which are held firmly in the jaws, whilst still resting solidly on the bench.

The jaws are fitted with replaceable cork and pigskin buffs to prevent bruising and damaging the work.

The carpenter's vice fitted to the side of the bench is useful for smaller jobs, but it does not stand up very well to the heavy banging necessary when roughing out larger pieces.

Each piece of work attempted will present its own individual problems. From start to finish, a number of methods may have to be used. Some of the problems call for ingenuity and inventiveness and the carver should not forget that an extra pair of hands often works wonders.

Carver's vice fitted with corks and leather buffs.

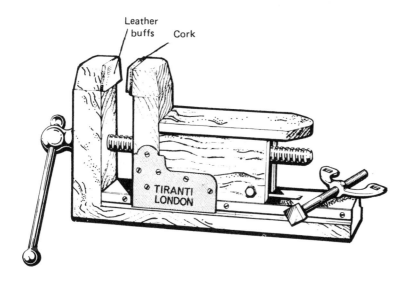

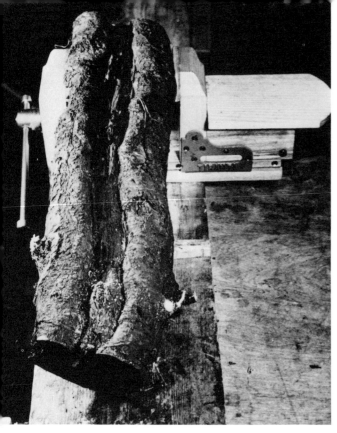

Carver's vice in use.

Chisels and Gouges

The selection of chisels and gouges will depend upon the type of work intended. A large collection is not necessary. Most sculptors are able to adapt and improvise tools to accomplish a wide variety of tasks.

Catalogues usually provide an illustrated description of the various sizes and sweeps of the tools. It is a good idea to start with six or seven tools selected to cover a wide range of duties. Additions may be made as the result of experience.

Tools are usually available already handled as required.

6

Straight	Bent	Back bent									
1	21										
2	22,23										
3	24	33									
4	25	34									
5	26	35									
6	27	36									
7	28	37									
8	29	38									
9	30										
10	31										
11	32										
39	43										
41	44										

Chisels Nos 1, 21   Corner chisels Nos 2, 22, 23   Gouges Nos 3-9, 24-30, 33-38

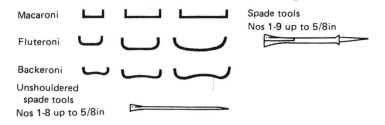

Macaroni

Fluteroni

Backeroni

Spade tools
Nos 1-9 up to 5/8in

Unshouldered
   spade tools
Nos 1-8 up to 5/8in

Catalogue description of chisels and gouges
Tool number, size, type, sweep and actual size of cuts are illustrated
(by courtesy Tiranti Ltd)

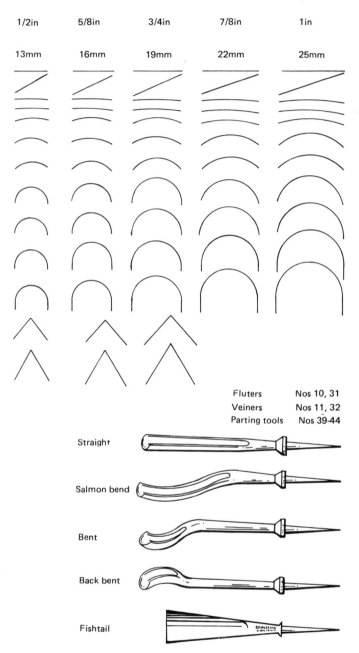

1/2in	5/8in	3/4in	7/8in	1in
13mm	16mm	19mm	22mm	25mm

Fluters	Nos 10, 31
Veiners	Nos 11, 32
Parting tools	Nos 39-44

Straight

Salmon bend

Bent

Back bent

Fishtail

Catalogue description of chisels and gouges (by courtesy Tiranti Ltd)

Brief Description of Chisels and Gouges *

Over many years the various tools have acquired names with which they are readily recognised, e.g. chisel, gouge, back bent gouge, etc.

Sizes vary a little with the type of tool but generally can be bought from $\frac{1}{16}$–1 in. Tools over 1 in wide may be a little difficult to handle for the beginner.

No. 1 Straight chisel Useful for some jobs such as chamfers. A skew chisel can also be used for this purpose.

No. 2 Skew chisel or slanting chisel Used for smoothing surfaces, cutting lines or chamfers. Also helpful for clearing out corners and acute crevices.

Nos. 3–5 Straight gouges This range has a fairly flat sweep. Useful for close modelling and refining the surface cuts.

Nos. 6–9 Straight gouges of medium sweeps Used for clearing rough surfaces, modelling forms, clearing backgrounds, etc.

No. 10 Fluter A gouge with a very deep sweep. Has steep sides and care should be taken not to work too deeply. Being a quick working tool it is useful for clearing work of all kinds, marking out and modelling certain forms.

No. 11 Veiner A straight sided tool with a deeply curved sweep at the bottom. Originally used for carving veined lines on foliage, etc.

Serves the same purpose as the Fluter.

Nos. 39 and 41 Parting tool Sometimes called a V-tool and extremely useful for marking out and lining, etc. Needs to be really well sharpened to work well.

---

* This has been compiled from the catalogue of Alec Tiranti Ltd and with their kind permission. The tool numbering system is that used in the catalogue.

9

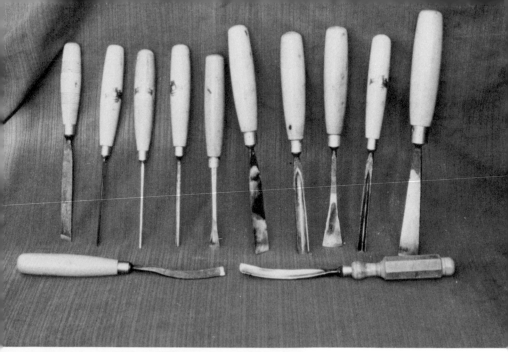

Twelve assorted tools.
From left to right: *Skew chisel; veiner (fine); very fine parting tool; very fine fluter; fish tail gouge (or spade tool); straight gouge (fine sweep); straight gouge (deep sweep or fluter); spade gouge; parting tool; allongee gouge; bent parting tool; bent gouge.*

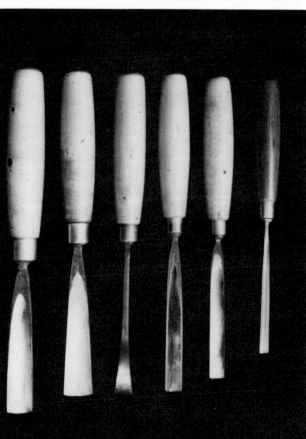

Gouges used for fine and medium heavy work.
From left to right: *fluter; straight gouge; parting tool; back-bent tool; allongee gouge; fluter.*

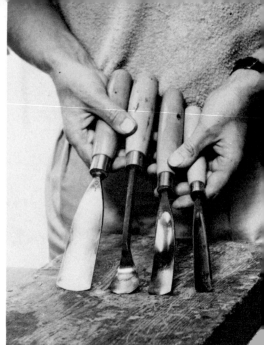

Gouges used for medium heavy work.
From left to right: *straight gouge; fluter; parting tool or* V-*tool; spade gouge; allongee gouge.*

Gouges used for heavy work.
From left to right: *boasting gouge, medium sweep; spoon-bit tool; bent gouge; fluter.*

Some chisels and gouges can be obtained as spade or fish-tail tools. This means that the blade narrows fairly quickly from the cutting edge to the handle, allowing the carver a clear working view and a lighter working tool.

Spade tools are extremely useful for all work demanding great accuracy, especially in the finishing process. They are not recommended for rough work or surface clearing. Most of the tools listed are also obtainable as 'bent' or 'back-bent'. These are specially shaped tools evolved for particular jobs.

11

Effect of a fluter with deep sweep. Cuts made across the grain.

Mallets of various shapes and weights: (left) *heavy lignum vitae;* (centre) *lightweight beech;* (right) *medium beech.*

Mallets

Wooden mallets are usually made of lignum vitae or beech and are supplied in various sizes and weights. Lignum vitae is by far the heaviest and harder wearing.

Carpenter's mallets can be used but are not really suitable. Metal mallets or hammers should *not* be used.

Select wooden mallets of suitable size and weight according to the power drive required.

When a model is nearing completion, it is necessary to proceed with more caution. A very light mallet or hand pressure is much more sensitive.

Rasps and Rifflers

Rasps and rifflers are used for shaping, rounding, refining or reducing waste wood where it is impractical for chisel or gouge work.

They are obtainable in various sizes, shapes and degree of cutting tooth from very fine to coarse.

Scrapers

May be bought, or they can be made quite easily from odd pieces of flexible spring steel. It is useful to have a varied selection of sizes, shapes, flats, curves and angles.

When correctly sharpened, they remove fine shavings and are valuable for preparing the surface of the work for finishing.

Additional Equipment

With time and experience, quite a number of additional tools and gadgets are acquired. These may not always be needed but are extremely useful from time to time, especially when one meets with difficulties.

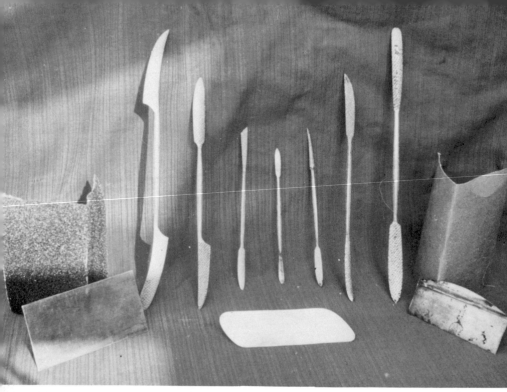

Tools for additional shaping and refining: rifflers of various sweeps and sizes; sandpaper of various grades; hand scrapers (metal) various shapes (edges sharpened).

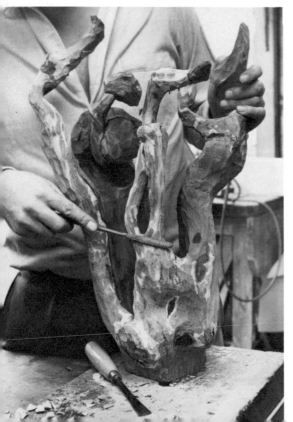

Use of riffler for shaping form in awkward places.

a) Use of the straight-edged metal hand scraper on flat timber surfaces.

b) The G-clamp is used to secure timber so that both hands are free.

c) Shaped scrapers are used to clear scratch marks. Select the scraper best suited to fit the shape of timber.

Splitting a large piece of timber using a metal wedge and hammer.

Sharpening and Care of Tools

Chisels and gouges are usually bought with the cutting edge already ground on the grindstone, but they are not sharpened. Before carving commences, the tools will need to be brought to a fine cutting edge. Dull cutting edges make comparatively easy tasks seem laborious and the finished result lacking in quality.

After a little practice, the beginner quickly acquires the knack of sharpening tools to a really fine cutting edge. A practical demonstration by a skilled person will save much wasted effort and prove invaluable experience. The carving of wood will constantly be interrupted by re-sharpening, so it is advisable to learn the correct methods from the very beginning.

Grinding

If the cutting edge of a gouge or chisel has been badly worn down, snipped or damaged, it will generally need re-grinding on a grindstone.

Care should be taken to ensure that the steel does not become overheated. To prevent this happening, it is advisable to either keep a constant flow of water over the grindstone or to dip the steel repeatedly into water whilst grinding.

Electrically-driven grindstones and Carborundum wheels – even of extra fine texture – are extremely quick working, so great care should be taken to keep the tool gently moving all the time.

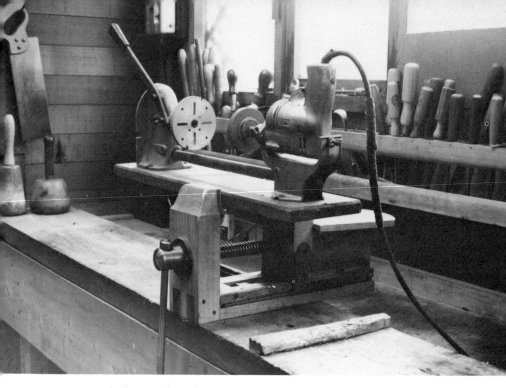

An inexpensive grindstone.

The approximate angle of a gouge when grinding.

Gouges differ from flat chisels in that they are curved or hollowed into a concave sweep and have a bevel on the outside of about 15° to the face. This angle is the result of the grinding process. To achieve the bevel, the grindstone is revolved away from the tool and the gouge is then firmly and steadily moved across the stone from side to side, constantly moving the position with a steady rolling action to prevent uneven wearing down. This is especially important near the centre and should continue until an even bevel of the correct angle results.

With care, accidents are not very frequent. If possible take your gouges to an expert for re-grinding until you are confident enough to attempt this operation yourself. A chisel or gouge should not be used for carving straight from the grindstone. It should first be sharpened to a keen cutting edge on an oilstone and slip.

Oilstones and Slips

A selection of these, varying in degree of coarseness, is essential. These are divided into natural stones, such as Washita, and artificial stones, such as 'India' and 'Carborundum'. Natural stones like Washita and Arkansas have the finest texture and are used to obtain the keenest cutting edge.

Carborundum and India stones are obtainable in fine, medium and coarse textures. Some are reversible. Fine on one side, medium or coarse on the other.

Slips are bought separately or in sets of varying shapes and sizes designed to fit the various gouge sweeps.

New oilstones and slips are best soaked in hot, fine oil for a few hours before first putting them into use.

The curved edges of slips should fit the gouge sweeps for which they are intended, and although they are apt to wear down, they can be kept in shape by rubbing down with coarse or medium sandpaper and finally the rubbing surface smoothed evenly with fine glasspaper, taking care

Sharpening slips in fine Carborundum. Sizes range from $6 \times 2\frac{1}{4} \times \frac{3}{4}-\frac{3}{8}$ in (top) *to $2\frac{1}{4} \times \frac{7}{8} \times \frac{1}{8}$ in* (bottom 3 forms).

to remove all trace of grit before using the slips for sharpening once again.

Oilstones and slips should always be placed on a level surface and made secure before use. Although quite durable, these stones are rather brittle and are certain to be badly damaged if they are dropped.

A good plan is to make a simple housing by fitting them onto a level piece of board wedged firmly into position with strips of wood glued to the board and fitting snugly to the sides of the stone to roughly half its depth. Repeated sharpening of gouges will wear grooves or hollows into the surface of the stone. Provision should be made so that the stone can be turned when the face is badly worn.

Various grades, sizes and shapes of oilstones and slips, with pig-skin leather strop (extreme right).

Sharpening

For one's first attempts at sharpening, a start should be made on a straight gouge with a fairly flat sweep, (No. 3 or No. 4 will be excellent for this purpose).

Place the oilstone or slip on a level surface, using a stop of some kind to prevent rocking and shifting. Soak the surface with a film of fine machine oil.

Then, place the edge to be sharpened on the stone at the desired angle, holding the handle firmly with the right hand and steadying the blade with the fingers of the left hand. With a slight rocking movement made with the right hand, start to slide the edge laterally along the stone from end to end, keeping an even movement and maintaining a steady pressure with the left hand. In this way the whole sweep is kept in contact with the stone at the correct angle.

Maintain the correct angle without elevating or depressing the handle. The gentle rocking movement assimilates

Approximate angle used for sharpening gouge of fairly flat sweep.

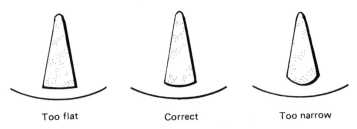

| Too flat | Correct | Too narrow |

Select the correct shape of sharpening slip to correspond with the curvature of the gouge.

the curve of the sweep. Increase the roll to accommodate the deeper arcs of the quicker cutting gouges.

Do not neglect the corners, otherwise the edges will soon hollow in the centre. Although the edge will be keen, the cutting quality will be impaired.

As the cutting edge develops, the displaced metal is pushed up on the inside hollow face causing a rough edge to appear. This rough surface can readily be detected by carefully sliding the fingers down the inside face of the gouge.

To remove this 'burr', as it is called, select a slip with a curved edge fitted to the hollow of the gouge. Place the gouge at a slightly upward incline on the edge of the bench, holding the handle with the left hand and the slip with the right hand. Oil the surface of the slip and place it flat along the inside face of the gouge, holding it upright so that the heel is held down flat against the inside shoulder of the tool. Using a firm, smooth pressure, slide the slip backwards and forwards so that it just clears the edge of the gouge. Continue this movement, gradually working across the face of the edge, taking care to maintain the forward and backward movement.

It is important to avoid rocking actions with the right hand, otherwise the edge quickly becomes rounded and a fresh start on the oilstone will be necessary.

Method of using a carborundum slip to remove the 'burr' and sharpen the inside edge of a gouge.

Use of a pig-skin leather strop, treated with strop dressing, for achieving very fine cutting edge on gouges and chisels.

Stropping

Finally, a few swift rubs on a leather strop, treated with a fine abrasive or strop-dressing, using the same rolling action as for the oilstone will remove any remaining burr and give the keenest cutting edge.

During the work of carving the cutting edge will occasionally lose its keenness. This may not be severe enough to merit resharpening on the oilstone. A few rubs on the strop may be all that is needed to regain the fine edge.

Differing Techniques

Veiners, parting tools, spoons and bent gouges, etc. require slightly different sharpening techniques. These may involve specially shaped and knife-edged slips designed to suit each individual tool. In the main, the principle involved in achieving a fine edge remains the same as already described for gouges.

After sharpening, always make a practice of wiping clean the oilstones and slips. Put them away in a safe place free from dust and grit.

Effects of grindstone and oilstone sharpening.

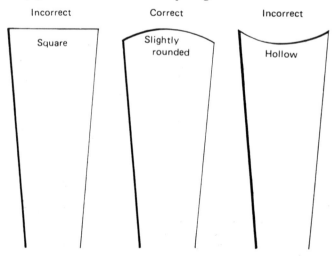

Incorrect   Correct   Incorrect

Square   Slightly rounded   Hollow

Basic Materials

Gathering together and building up a small timber store of carving material can be a delightful source of satisfaction and enjoyment. Apart from one's own efforts, very little expense need be incurred.

It is a distinct advantage to have a store of good carving timber set aside awaiting the opportune moment for carving.

The size of the store will depend upon available space and the scope and extent of the work intended, ranging from a few small pieces of carefully selected material stacked away under the bench to a more ambitious arrangement outdoors.

Wood for carving should be well seasoned and kept in cool, airy conditions, protected from rain and hot sun.

Acquiring Carving Material

Collecting and searching for suitable carving wood can be fun, full of interest and the excitement of making discoveries in the most unlikely places.

A good source for useful offcuts are timber yards, where logs are rough sawn into boards and planks.

Beams and timber fittings, especially from old property under demolition, provide useful material together with reclaimed wood from old furniture, doors, staircases and disused fence posts.

Learn to recognise timbers both in the log and sawn states, especially for their working qualities.

Woodland walks are likely to be fruitful, especially in winter when the grass has died down exposing many interesting broken-off pieces which would remain hidden in summer. Never take pieces from a living tree.

25

Places to look for interesting carving material.

26

Weathered and well-seasoned timber (laburnum) ideal for carving imaginative and interesting forms.

Streams, lakes and windswept moorlands are good hunting grounds for material suitable for carving interesting and unusual shapes and forms. Broken pieces of green or sappy wood will take considerable time seasoning before being fit for carving, so there is no need to damage healthy growing trees. However, keep a sharp lookout for logs that have recently been felled, either intentionally, blown down by gales or uprooted by soil erosion. Of course, permission should always be obtained before removing any timber from woodland.

Decayed wood is useless for carving, although some good pieces can be sorted out. Removal of the decayed parts will often reveal sound timber underneath.

Avoid worm or grub infested wood, also timber which feels soft and spongy.

Weatherworn, misshapen trunks, branches and roots should not escape attention.

Much valuable material is to be found in cities, towns and villages, neglected or deserted gardens, old property, churchyards, junk shops and timber stores may provide useful sources of valuable material.

A knowledge of tree recognition is worth developing. It is surprising how quickly interest is awakened and deeper insight is gleaned with actual contact with the living forms and a knowledge of the natural environment.

Carving Qualities of Some Timbers

Alder (Common)

The wood is greenish-white, turning reddish-brown after seasoning. Reasonably soft and works easily. Smooths down well and takes a good finish.

Found pieces of mountain (scrub) oak suitable for carving natural forms. The rhythm of the natural forms and run of the grain are clearly defined.

Ash

Heartwood is pinkish or black in colour. Tends to be a little coarse, but works well and takes a good finish.

Apple

Soft working and close grained. Takes a good finish.

Beech

Light brown colour. Hard and usually with a close straight grain. Fine texture and very durable. Works quite well but lacks good finish.

Birch (European)

Whitish to pale brown in colour. Fairly straight grained. Medium-hard and close-textured. Easy to work. Takes good finish.

Large baulk of timber (pitch pine), split by wedging into manageable size. Notice the very straight run of the grain, ideal for splitting with wedges.

Boxwood

Rich ivory colour. Fine-grained and durable. Works well and takes a good finish.

Cherry (European)

Reddish colour. Fine even texture, fairly straight grain. Works well and takes a good finish. Tends to darken with age.

Chestnut (Sweet or Spanish)

When worked it closely resembles oak, but is much lighter in weight and does not have the silver grain. Light brown

Suitable types of timber for carving should be stored in cool, airy, dry conditions. At front, from left to right: *mountain oak (natural form); oak (sawn from the log); rosewood (sawn to show colour and grain); English yew (sawn to show colour and grain); sycamore (sawn to show colour and grain); oak 12th century (sawn from demolished church column).* Horizontally lying: *laburnum (split by wedging).* Back: *afromosia (plank).*

in colour. Fairly straight, close-grained. Easy to work and finish. *Horse Chestnut* has little value for carving.

Cedar

Fine-grained softwood. Light and easy to work. Colour varies from light straw to dark brown.

Elm

Heartwood light brown to reddish. Light yellow sapwood. Often cross-grained making it difficult to work. Coarse-grained but often with good figure. Takes a good finish.

Wych Elm

Paler in colour than common elm. Is straighter grained making it easier working.

Ebony (Africa, Indonesia)

Very heavy, close-grained and durable. Colour from black to greenish yellow. Sometimes streaked. Good finish.

Holly

Heartwood creamy white. Moderately hard. Close-grained. Light in weight.

Laburnum

Heartwood varies considerably from light buff to dark brown. Golden yellow sapwood. Close grained medium hard and durable. Good smooth finish.

Lime

Colour yellowish-white tending to turn a light buff with seasoning. Straight, close-grained. Cuts well in all directions. Fairly soft and easy working.

Lignum Vitae (Cuba, Bahamas, South America)

Very heavy, hard and durable. Difficult to carve because of its hardness. Close-grained and compact. Heartwood varies in colour from light green to almost black. Sapwood is creamy coloured and hard enough to be included in the carving.

Mahogany (West Indies, South America, Africa)

Medium weight. Durable. Colour varies from shades of yellow to rich reddish brown. Fine-grained and smooths well to a very good finish.

Maple

Heartwood varies from light buff to reddish-brown. Compact and close-grained. Medium hard. Takes a good finish.

Oak

Varieties include Japanese, American White and European, Slavonian, Polish and English. Each has distinctive features, and variations in colour, figure and weight.

Generally hard, well figured and extremely durable. Works well and takes good finish.

Pine (Many Varieties)

Soft to medium hardness, depending on variety. Some resinous. Many variations in colour from creamy white to reddish-browns. Grain varies considerably. Liable to contain numerous knots.

Purple Heart (Cuba, Guianas)

Purple to reddish-brown in colour. Hard, close-grained and durable. Takes a fine polish.

Rosewood (Africa, Brazil, East Indies, Honduras)

Even-textured timber with beautiful colouring and figure. Colour varies considerably through dark purples, reddish-browns and streaky blacks. Medium to heavy working. Smooths to a very fine finish.

One method of transporting useful timber!

Sycamore

Whitish in colouring tending to turn pale brown. Fine, even grain. Finishes to a smooth surface.

Occasionally, wavy-grained which presents an attractive ripple.

Teak (India, Java, Burma, Ceylon, Africa)

Colour varies from light yellow to light brown. Hard, even grain sometimes subject to tearing. Durable. Takes a good finish.

Walnut

Many varieties including English, French, American, Italian, Spanish. Colour and grain differ but generally it varies from rich purplish brown to a greyish background streaked with dark brown.

Works well and is hard and durable. Takes a fine, smooth finish.

Yew

Fine-grained, hard and durable. Heartwood reddish-brown. Sapwood creamy white. Good figure and interesting run of grain. Smooths to a fine surface and takes a good finish.

Carved Platters, Dishes and Bowls

Platters

Cutting the flattened shapes and slightly hollowed contours involved in the making of platters helps the beginner to acquire some knowledge of the working qualities of different timbers and also the feel of some of the tools employed for this work.

Dishes and Bowls

Hand-carved dishes and bowls offer an interesting challenge for the next step, which embraces a stronger emphasis on design and more skilful handling of a wider range of tools.

Many beautiful examples, both decorative and functional, are to be found in great variety. It is a fascinating study to trace their history and development throughout the ages.

Function and Design

Before making a start, the type and size of bowl required should be given some consideration.

If the bowl is to be used for a specific purpose, e.g. a fruit bowl, salad bowl, etc. then the functional use must be of prime importance and should be blended into the design, so that the finished product is not only useful but also present a pleasing and attractive appearance.

The size will naturally depend upon the wood available. The design should be entirely individual and personal. The natural contours and grain of the wood must be carefully studied and taken into account when working out the design.

Form and Shape

Types of bowls can be roughly divided into three main groups:

Flat shallow platters and dishes stressing outline and which are only slightly hollowed. The shape may vary from severe straight lines or simple curves to more complicated flowing forms.
Formal which are of regular or formal design.
Formed making greater use of the natural movements and features suggested by the timber.

The design may not necessarily be restricted to any one of these groups. There can often be combinations, although at the outset it is important to decide what is intended.

A number of elements will now have to be considered.

Grain

The way the grain moves or lies within the wood should be studied and a mental picture formed of the finished piece. The final appearance can be affected by the contours formed during carving and a straight grain can be made more rhythmic by intentionally carving a series of undulating valleys and hills.

The working properties of the grain should be carefully noted. Intricate and tricky passages in design are best kept clear of the end grain until a really skilful use of tools has been acquired. The eccentric meanderings of the grain in some timbers are difficult to visualise without patience, study and understanding. This ability to visualise can

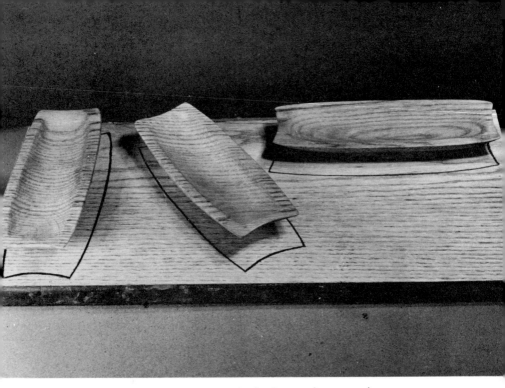

Three shallow dishes carved from same plank of sweet chestnut, using a template for positioning of shape. Varying the position of the outline in relation to the run of the grain affects the appearance of the finished form. (left) Template outline placed across grain at right angles. (centre) Template outline placed diagonally across grain. (right) Template outline placed lengthways along run of grain.

only be acquired through practice and familiarity with the materials. It is advisable in the early stages to restrict the carvings to timbers having a regular grain which will work evenly in all directions. Lime is especially recommended for this purpose.

Colour

There are many very beautiful self- and multi-coloured timbers available. The colour of the wood should be integrated within the design, so that other qualities are not overshadowed or completely lost.

The ideal is a harmonious marrying of form, grain,

colour and texture – to produce a well balanced piece of work where each element can be seen to its best advantage. Every opportunity should be taken to study the work of experts and to notice particularly the sensitivity and subtle artistry in the use of these various qualities.

Ideas for Design

In nature, we have the perfect source of reference for the personal study and development of form and colour. There is an endless array of beauty displayed in many wonderful facets. One can do no better than to observe and study more closely the common examples we usually take so much for granted.

Stages in carving a shallow platter from a disused chair seat (sweet chestnut):
1 The shape of the outline is marked with soft chalk. Make use of as much available timber as possible. This reduces unnecessary carving with a minimum of waste.
2 Method of removing large areas of waste by use of a hand saw.

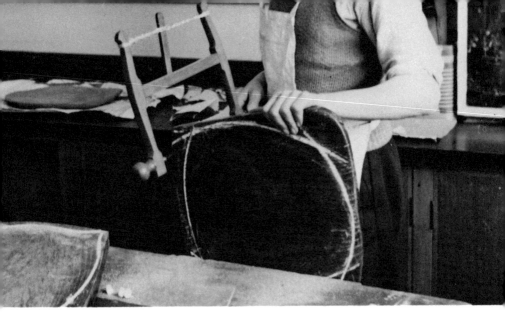

3 *A bow-saw is used to remove waste material.*

4 *Trimming the edges to achieve the marked shape. A spokeshave or a gouge with a flat sweep can be used for this purpose. Sometimes a wood rasp will prove very effective.*

5 Place the work firmly on bench and secure with a G-clamp and wooden block. Use a gouge of medium sweep to clear the waste, working from outside edges, across the grain and towards the centre. Avoid a curvature which is too steep. Keep centre fairly high at this stage. Hand pressure or a light-weight mallet may be used to drive the gouge.

6 The centre point of balance and base area are marked on the underside with soft chalk. A gouge of medium sweep is used to clear the waste, working outwards from the centre across the grain. Curvature should be taken into consideration and carefully judged. Hand pressure or a lightweight mallet can be used to drive the gouge. Secure the work against a firm wood block fixed to the bench. A G-clamp may be used for difficult parts (see Stage 3). Care should be taken to place the G-clamp so that cracks do not occur as a result of pressure on the wood.

7 *Use a gouge of fairly flat sweep to complete the shaping and to refine the surface texture. Secure the work firmly to the bench and use hand pressure to drive the gouge.*

During the course of the four seasons, the shapes of leaves provide an abundant source of inspiration for the enquiring and imaginative mind. Other areas which may be explored are the numerous varieties of shape and form derived from many fruits and vegetables, both wild and cultivated, during their different stages of development. Nature should provide countless ideas for adaptation.

Drawing and Sketching Ideas for Design

During the making of any particular piece, the expert is able to see the finished image quite clearly within the timber throughout the various stages of its development. It requires only an occasional mark to indicate a prominent feature. The secret lies in constantly training both eye and mind to visualise carving in three dimensions, or in

8 *The finished platter. Coated with heat-resistant and water-proof sealer. This prevents unsightly water markings and discoloration.*

the round, as it is sometimes called. This takes considerable practice and the beginner will need to resort to marking out his ideas first on paper and then on the surface of the wood. From the very beginning, it is better to draw freehand, using a very soft pencil or chalk which can be easily erased if not satisfactory. Great skill in drawing is not necessary. It is surprising how quickly the facility to sketch or rough out an idea develops after a little practice.

Ideas for design are best tried out on paper first, allowing alternative ideas to emerge until a satisfactory outline or general shape is established. The most important aspect will be the impression evolving in the mind's eye.

Cut-outs, or templates, as they are called, are quite

useful especially for accurate reproductions, but their use is limited. Every endeavour should be made to acquire the freshness and vitality of direct freehand drawing from the very beginning.

A dish of flowing, informal design (laburnum).

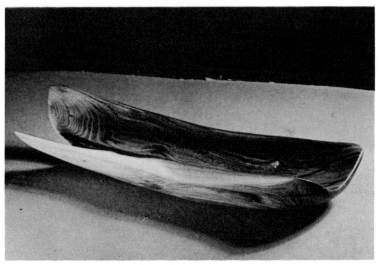

A shallow bowl of informal design. The shape is suggested by natural contours and texture of sawn elm burr.

Stages in carving a
bowl of formal design
(*sycamore*).
1 Initial marking out
in soft chalk from
pencil sketch.
Unwanted off-cuts
are removed with a
handsaw.

2 The centre and base
area are marked in
chalk. Work from
each end in turn with
gouges of flat to
medium sweep used
where necessary.

3 The handle areas are
drilled to allow gouge
clearance.

4 *Waste material from handle areas is removed with a fluter gouge. Work proceeds from either side in turn to meet at the middle.*

5 *Handle areas are cleaned and developed using a gouge of fairly flat sweep, a spokeshave and a riffler.*

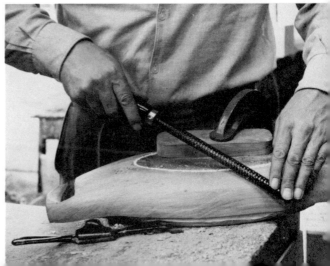

6 *Refining the curved areas, using a Surform rasp and a spokeshave.*

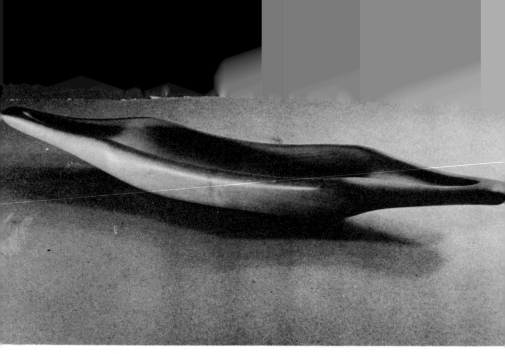

A shallow dish of formal design (alder).

A shallow bowl (afromosia wood) of formal design with a smooth polished finish. The shallow depression is left textured from the gouge cuts.

Finishes for Platters, Dishes and Bowls

The correct finish for completed work always demands thoughtful care.

Attention should be given to the purpose or function of the model. This is of prime importance. A particular work may look at its best if left direct from the chisel or gouge, whilst others are enhanced by a very smooth, polished appearance.

Occasionally, a mixing of both chiselled texture, blended with areas which are smoothly polished can present interesting highlights.

The final choice of a finish remains with the carver.

Tooled finishes produce pleasing contrasts of light and shadow, varying with the differing directions of the gouge cuts.

A shallow platter (sweet chestnut) of informal design with division. Various grades of sandpaper are used to remove gouge marks and scratches, to show the natural colour and the run of grain to full advantage.

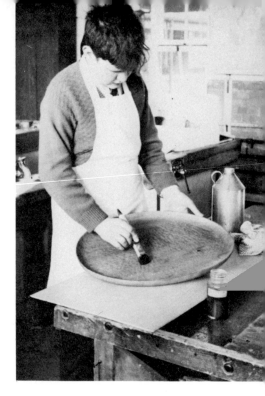

Two or three thin coats of heat-resistant and water-proof lacquer will seal the surface and produce a durable matt or glossy finish, enhancing texture, natural colour and appearance of grain.

Chisels and gouges should be very sharp for the best results.

A light rubbing down with very fine glasspaper is all that will be required for completion.

For smooth-polished finishes, it is necessary to remove all gouge and scratch marks from the surface with great care. Fine-toothed rifflers and various grades of sandpaper are used to accomplish this task. The work is often tedious, but the highly polished result proves well worth the time and effort expended.

Platters, dishes and bowls are meant to be useful and so will obviously receive much handling and wear. They are also subject to discoloration if the surface is not protected. Platters used for foodstuffs (salads, etc.) need to be oiled regularly before and after use with fine olive oil which is

A large bowl of informal design (English cherry). A fine glossy finish results from the application of a few coats of wax polish.

applied thinly and finally wiped over with a clean, dry cloth.

In some cases, it may be advisable to seal the surface pores of the wood against heat and water. Two or three thin coats of the sealing lacquer should be applied evenly and, when dry, lightly rubbed down with fine glasspaper.

This treatment will also bring out the subtle qualities of natural colouring, run of grain and details of forms.

If the dish or bowl is not intended to hold perishable fruits or other foodstuffs, a thin coat of white wax polish can be applied evenly, well rubbed in and brought to a high sheen with a clean soft duster. This will present a highlighted model of lasting appearance. Lacquering and wax polishing are best done under warm conditions.

Artificial staining of the wood is not necessary.

Natural Form and the Imaginative Use of Wood

Basic Qualities of Wood

Before carving commences, the piece of wood intended for use should be examined carefully and one should note the various peculiarities which contribute towards the individuality of the particular piece of wood.

This 'reading the wood', as it is often called, consists of estimating the movement of the grain and imagining its surface appearance where unwanted wood will be removed and where penetrations will take place during the carving.

Grain

A term referred to a good deal in woodworking. Briefly, it means the arrangement of cellular fibres which produce an image or 'figure' as it is called, on the surface of the wood.

These fibres lie in bundles running throughout the whole length of the timber.

When the wood is cut across the grain, ends of each of these tube-like fibres can be seen. This is the *end grain*.

Knowledge of the grain is necessary, not only for anticipating appearance but also for the cutting which should run with the grain or across it . . . not against it.

Hardwoods and Softwoods

Timber for woodworking is divided chiefly into two main groups, but there are other wood features to be considered.

Hardwoods

Woods obtained from broad leaved trees, e.g. Oak, Ash, Beech, Sycamore, etc.

Softwoods

These are obtained from coniferous trees, (Pines etc.) and are usually much lighter in weight.

Bark

This is the outer protective covering. Apart from a few exceptions, it is of little use for carving.

Sapwood

The recent growth, usually containing moisture or sap.

Cross-section of an elm trunk.

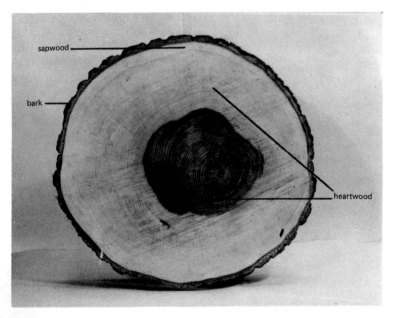

Heartwood

Generally harder, denser and a richer colour than sap-wood. Most timbers, provided they are not decayed or infected throughout, can be carved successfully into interesting and imaginative forms. There is a great range of timbers which are ideal for carving. Some are much easier to work than others and the beginner will be much safer working a few of the well-known kinds.

Figure

This describes markings on the wood caused by the grain. Figure can vary considerably in its appearance. Effects of branch formation, wind, colour, size and the arrangement of cellular structure all contribute to the figured appearance of timbers.

Texture

The size and formation of the fibres determines the texture. Oak and Ash are fairly coarse textured, whilst Maple is classed as a fine texture.

Abnormal Figure and Burrs

Occurring in wood as a result of old wounds which have calloused over. They may often be the result of irregular growth due to high winds or, more often, through the activities of insect infection. Some insect infections penetrate the bark, stimulating the growing cells to increase division. This results in a mixing of the new wood with the bark and causes a swelling of wartlike appearance on the trunks and branches of certain trees. Some species of the trees are more susceptible than others.

When sawn, these 'burrs' often produce features of beautiful appearance.

Several examples of small elm burrs. These provide interesting examples of eccentric colour and grain.

Small dishes and shallow bowls carved from sawn elm burrs. The natural features have been retained and used in the informal designs.

Stages in carving a sculpture using exposition and development of existing natural forms and features:

1 The original laburnum trunk. The base is sawn to establish the point of balance.
2 Removal of the bark using a gouge of medium sweep.
3 The bark removed. The piece can now be thoroughly examined to discover its qualities and most interesting features.

Stages in Carving Natural Forms

Natural Forms and Found Pieces

1 Clean away all loose moss and soil especially from holes and between cracks. If necessary, wash the piece thoroughly with clear water and allow to dry out slowly. If there is a clear running stream nearby much of this work can be done on the spot before transporting to the store or workshop.

2 Using various tools and scrapers. Remove all areas of decay and infection.

3 Carefully examine the natural run of the grain.

4 Notice prominent features and areas of particular interest.

5 Try to visualise a mental map of the existing undulations and pleasing sweeps of form.

4 Clearing of waste and preliminary development of penetrations. Gouges of medium sweep and fluters are useful for this work.

5 Development and refining of surface areas and interesting features.

6 Establish base or points of balance.

7 Explore natural holes and penetrations. Determine where modifications need be made.

8 When the piece is clean and dry, start carving by following the run of the grain. Try to let the grain determine the run of the tool, both along and across the undulations and hollows.

9 Use imagination and individual sense of design to enhance the natural features and develop less interesting areas.

10 Endeavour to view the piece as a whole or completely in the round.

11 Try to establish a harmonious sense of proportion between the solid masses and the overall rhythm in relation to grain and colour.

The finished three-dimensional sculpture, wax polished.

A piece of laburnum suggesting two forms joined and the finished piece resulting in a twisting form to give a suggestion of movement and relationship.

58

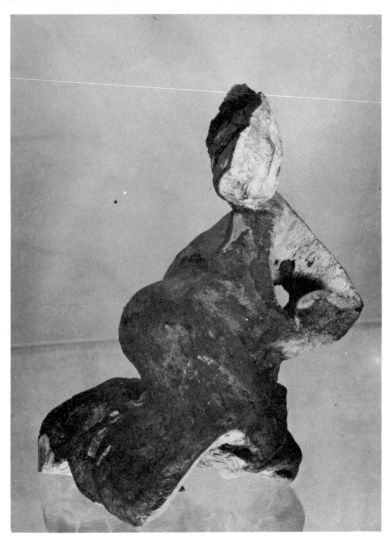

A found piece (birch) suggesting a kneeling figure.

12 Some found pieces already present definite represen-
    tational appearances (fish, animal forms, figures,
    heads, etc.). The originality of such pieces can be
    most interesting and exciting. As much of the natural
    formation and appearance should be retained,
    although some improvisation may be necessary.

13 When carving and shaping is completed, the kind of
    finish most appropriate should be determined.

Development of large vertical natural form from a piece of mountain (scrub) oak. Gouges and fluters of medium and deep sweeps used to follow and refine natural hollows and contours. Gouge marks and run of the tool accentuate the rhythm and suggest movement. Textured finish highlights the form with light and shadow.

Finished sculpture, waxed and polished. Note the natural two-tone colour effect.

Vertical form carved from very old English yew.

Formal design in oak, with multiple penetrations.

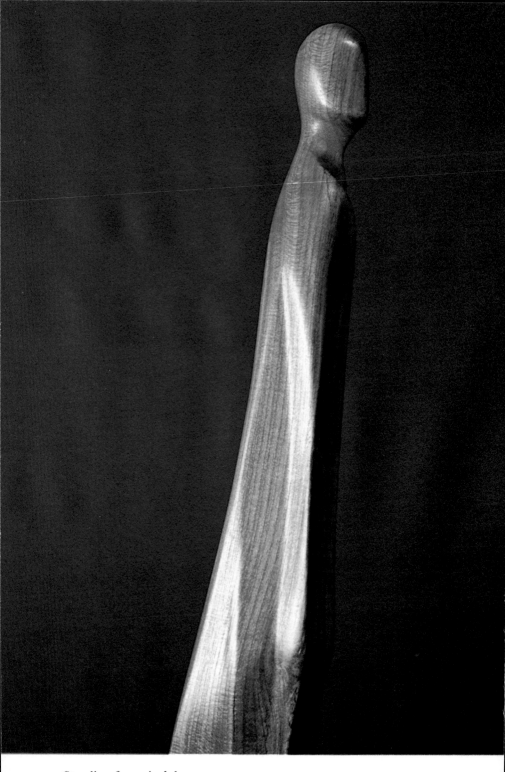

Standing figure in laburnum.

14 The kind of finish will largely depend upon the size of the piece and whether it is to stand outdoors or be utilised as indoor decoration.

For sculptures which will be displayed outdoors, some form of protective coating will be necessary, e.g. teak oil or some form of waterproof lacquer.

For use indoors, the sculpture may be left as finished direct from the tooling, which gives a pleasing textured appearance. For more subtle presentation, the piece can be further refined by rubbing down to a smooth finish using various grades of sandpaper. A few thin coats of wax polish, well brushed into the surface, should produce a matt or glossy finish as required.

A seasoned elm burr, cut from tree. The interesting natural features have been retained and developed.

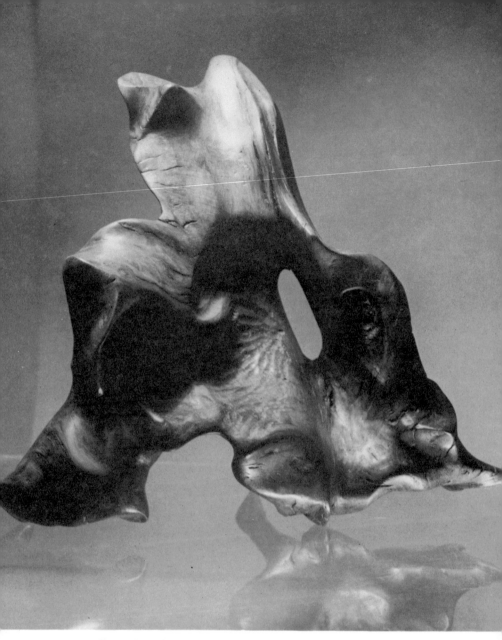

Example of flowing penetrated form, refined and polished (mountain oak).

Carving Abstracts

The object of carving abstracts is to produce sculptures representing ideas in geometric and other designs. These may be of a formal or informal nature, angular, flowing or combinations of these elements.

The ideas may be initially inspired by nature, but the shaping of the forms becomes personalised by incorporating one's own fantasies, variations and improvisations. Ideas vary from very simple expressions to highly complex representations.

The carving of abstracts requires boldness of purpose and approach. With practice, the ability to visualise the graceful beauty of outline and masses develops into a greater sensitivity towards the basic materials and equipment involved.

By allowing unrestricted use of imaginative ideas, one may also develop a feeling of seeing beyond the superficial surface appearances.

Form, colour, grain and rhythm are fused and blended to produce a harmonious whole. Each element is of equal importance. Before carving, careful consideration should be given to each so that a successful marriage of all the elements is effected. It is noticeable when one element is singing a different song.

Full or partial penetrations may provide distinctive focal points and added interest. Penetrations, either single or multiple, often invest the sculpture with a feeling of lightness and elegance where the graduated shadows lend a sense of mystery to the spatial and rhythmic qualities of the form.

*Stages in carving an
abstract form of
informal design with
a single penetration
(walnut):*

1 *The timber is cut
to a suitable size
and the base estab-
lished.*

2 *Gouges of fairly
flat and medium
sweeps used to
prepare rough
outer surface.*

3 *The basic shape and point of balance are now established. A single penetration is required to remove the unsightly knot.*

4 *From an outside perimeter, a fluter is used for working towards a centre, for the positioning of penetration.*

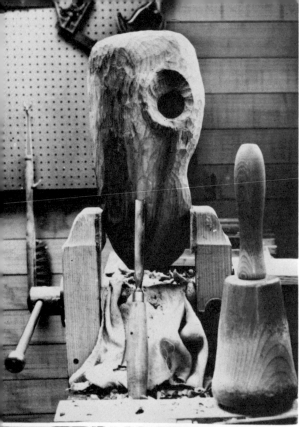

5 Gouges and fluters
of suitable size
and sweeps are
used to make the
penetration from
the opposite side.
Both penetrations
should meet at a
centre to form a
complete single
penetration.

6 The final shaping
and refinement of
form and penetra-
tion is accom-
plished with
gouges of flat
sweep and rifflers
of differing sizes,
shapes and cutting
tooth.
All the surfaces
are cleaned of tool
and scratch marks
using a hand
scraper and sand-
paper of various
grades.

7 A final coating of
a thinly applied
mixture of bees-
wax and American
turpentine will
result in a satin
finish of fine sheen.
The wax finish
helps to preserve
the wood and
minimise any
discoloration
resulting from
frequent handling.
Repolish whenever
necessary.

8 The completed
abstract form.

*Vertical formal design
with spiral
(mahogany).*

*A rounded, informal design accen-
tuating the flow of the grain in
relation to forms (pine).*

A formal geometric design with single penetration (afromosia).

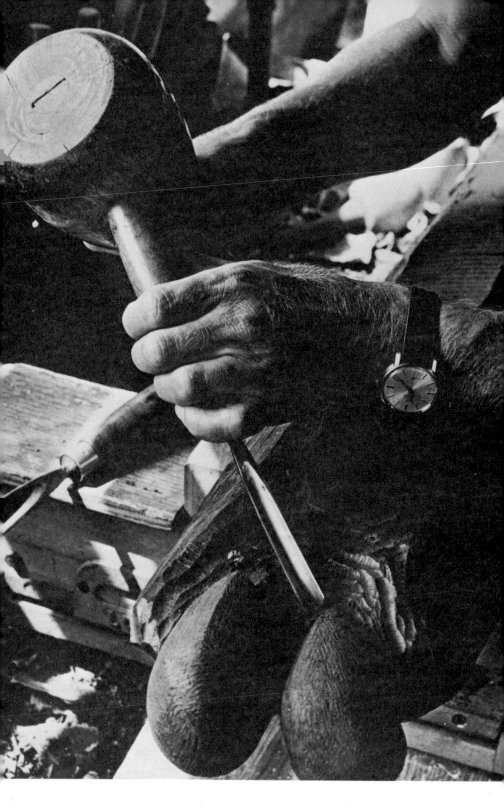

Abstract Figurative Carving in the Round

High and Low Relief carvings have a background and are ingeniously designed to be viewed from frontal angles. These works are two-dimensional, consisting of connecting masses and lines combined with the technique of perspective to create effects depending largely on light and shade.

'Carving in the round' is three-dimensional. The sculpture being of equal importance when viewed from all angles, whether it be fully abstract or figurative in design.

Abstract figurative representations carved fully in the round depend upon the arrangement of masses, proportions and their rhythms to form a harmonious whole. This presents a creative challenge which is vital, interesting and instructive. It is essential that the carver learns to visualise the whole arrangement, first within his mind's eye, and then to transpose this to suitably selected material for development. When the most suitable piece of timber has been selected, it is advisable to spend some considerable time examining and studying the nature of the wood until a clear conception becomes fixed in the mind. Sketches and drawings are two-dimensional and are of little help in the actual carving, either on paper or drawn on the wood to be carved. Experimental models in plastic materials (clay, plaster, etc.) may give some general indications and familiarisation with the overall general idea, but at best they are second-hand and the carving may be in danger of becoming a copy or replica of the model and thus lose the natural individuality of the wood. However, some experience of the importance and relationship of the main masses and details may be

71

Opposite: *The author carving a unified couple.*

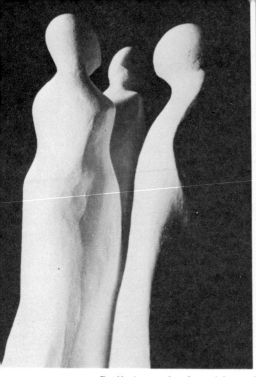

Preliminary sketch models made prior to actual wood carving in order to give some indication of the basic idea, rhythms, proportions and the relationship of the main masses: clay model of small integrated female figure group (above left), *model in plaster of a single figure* (above right), *model in plaster of integrated male figure group* (below left), *Plasticine model of composite group of female figures* (below right).

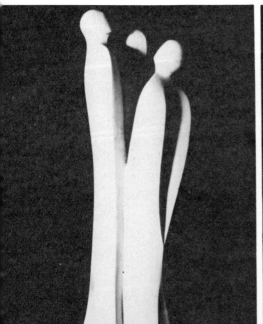
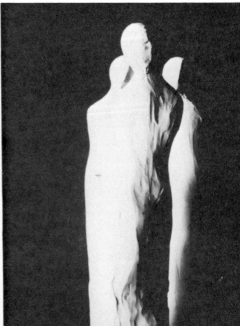

gained, especially if one allows the spontaneity and freedom for personal experimentation, exploration of possibilities and improvisation.

When 'carving in the round' the wood should be viewed carefully from every aspect and mental notes made of the particular qualities inherent in the wood, both visible and those which so often lie hidden within the timber. Previous experience of carving natural forms will prove invaluable practice and first rate experience for learning to 'read the wood' and how to visualise.

During the initial 'reading of the wood', endeavour to establish the main focal points of interest, appearance of the grain and where detailed passages or simplifications may be established and be most effective.

By the time carving commences, a good clear picture of the finished sculpture should have been formed in the mind. Keep a sharp look out for imperfections in the timber, e.g. knots, cracks, etc., places where the main difficulties may arise. Inventiveness and improvisation can incorporate these defects effectively into the finished work. Indeed, abnormalities in the wood may be utilised positively to form most interesting features. The open-minded carver may even design a whole sculpture to good advantage utilising a particular defect in the wood and making the defect the most prominent feature, instead of trying to work around or even hide the imperfection.

Make every effort to preserve and incorporate into the overall design as much of the natural characteristics of the timber as possible. Avoid being too dominant and obsessed with your own concept. Let nature guide you and do as much of the work as possible. Nature is the best teacher of the creative carver and much can be learned through happy accidents. Aim for an agreeable marriage between your own ideas and the possibilities offered by the timber. Try to give equal importance to all details within the work as a whole. The carving techniques used in abstract figurative sculptures can best be comprehended by studying the series of illustrations sequence included in this chapter.

It will be seen that the bulk of the carving is accomplished using relatively few tools and implements and that a large range and variety of expensive gouges are not necessary. With growing experience, one tool can be adapted to do successfully the job of a number of other tools which have been specially designed to accomplish one particular task. Every carver has his own particular favourite set of tools, which are invariably brought into use for almost every carving.

In figure carving, there are certain basic principles involved and although the order of working may vary, the same principles generally apply.

Some carvers start at the top of the model and work downwards, others start at the bottom and work upwards, whilst others prefer working around the piece. No matter which way is employed, the complete image of the finished work needs to be kept in mind. In this way sure and confident cutting is assured and tentative attempts ('mouse nibbling') are avoided.

Only with practice, experiment and comparison of methods and results will the surety of execution and expression develop.

When first starting to carve a piece of sculpture fully in the round, it is advisable to select a good, sound piece of hardwood of manageable size and proportions. A piece 10–12 in high, of 3–4 in diameter and free from cracks and knots will be ideal. If the piece is too small the work may become cramped and fussy when carved by beginners. If too large the work may seem too slow and tedious resulting in loss of interest.

Before commencing actual carving, carefully examine the piece of wood for defects. Square off the base with a handsaw and mark the estimated point of balance on the base with a soft piece of chalk.

Stages in figure carving, fully in the round – the stages are fully described in the accompanying main text.

Stages in Carving Figures Fully in the Round

Progressions involved in carving two integrated figures (couple carving).
Wood: Purple heart (Amaranth).

1 After careful scrutiny, the timber is firmly fixed in the vice at an easy working angle.
2 Approximate angles and positions of heads are marked on the top end grain.

   A $\frac{1}{2}$-in fluter gouge is used for roughing out around the heads to explore the run of the grain and establish position of the heads.

3 Unwanted wood is cleared from around heads, leaving plenty of material for later refinement. The initial position for later separation of the heads is then marked.

Equipment used for 1–3

A ¼-inch fluter or veining gouge, a ⅝-in parting tool, a ½-in gouge or spade gouge of medium sweep, a ½-in fluter gouge.

4   The inclination of heads is marked, followed by careful clearing around both heads and shoulders using a $\frac{1}{2}$-in fluter. The uppermost separation between heads is effected to determine proportions and distinguish between male and female.

Equipment used for 4

A $\frac{1}{2}$-in fluter gouge, a $\frac{5}{8}$-in parting tool, a $\frac{3}{8}$-in gouge or spade gouge of medium sweep, a $\frac{1}{4}$-in veiner or fluter gouge for quick and fine cutting.

5   Initial shaping of the body forms using a $\frac{1}{2}$-in fluter
    gouge and a $\frac{3}{4}$-in straight or fish-tail gouge. Careful
    exploration of qualities and possibilities within tim-
    ber, e.g. run of the grain, colour, imperfections.

Equipment used for 5

   A $\frac{1}{2}$-in fluter gouge, a $\frac{5}{8}$-in straight or spade gouge and
   a parting tool for clearance and shoulder separation.

6 Fuller separation of the heads in relation to shoulder inclinations.

The approximate position of chest levels are marked in chalk and kept fairly high at this stage.

Main emphasis around attitudes and angles of heads, with only light clearing around shoulders and chest levels.

Additional equipment for head and shoulder working

In addition to the tools used previously, rifflers of varying sizes, shapes and cuts are invaluable, especially around the heads and shoulders on the end grain, where gouge carving may prove very difficult.

79

7   Establishment of the main body masses of both figures, leaving suggestions for later details.

8   Gradual shaping of both male and female forms proceeds simultaneously. The more prominent high

points are revealed. The rhythm of the shoulder attitudes in relation to the suggested arm positions is of prime importance and some wood should be left for later refinement.

9   Development of body forms in relation to heads and shoulders. Refinement of body masses using a $\frac{1}{2}$-in fish-tail gouge and spokeshave. Much care should be taken when using a spokeshave.

10 Final positioning and defining of arm details.
Much care is needed for this process to ensure that all other elements, e.g. heads, shoulders, breasts and other body contours are proportional and relate harmoniously.

Equipment used for 10

Rifflers of various sizes, shapes and cuts are most useful for the delicate shaping.

11 Further refining of heads, shoulders and the larger body masses as the suggested details now become more apparent. Again, a range of varying rifflers will prove a great asset when reaching some of the more inaccessible places.

83

12 All deep scratch marks are removed with a metal
hand scraper and coarse-grade sandpaper.

13 More detailed refinement, paying particular attention to the more subtle aspects of the various forms.
The work should proceed carefully by hand, covering
very small areas.

As at all stages in the development, it is important
frequently to view the sculpture from many angles as
the work proceeds.

Use well-worn, coarse-grade sandpaper for this
operation.

14 The smaller and more minute scratch marks are

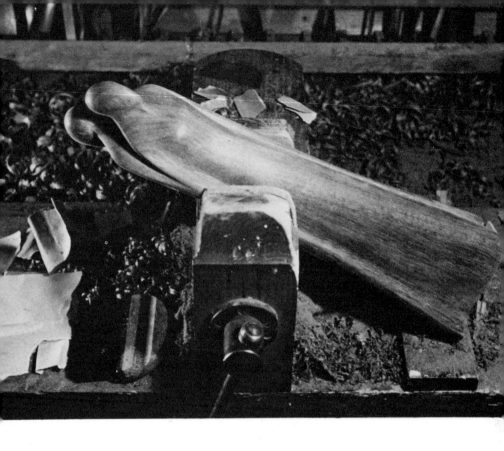

removed using a medium-grade sandpaper with a
final smoothing of all surfaces using worn glasspaper.
15 When all tiny scratch marks have been removed with
very fine glasspaper, the surface wood should have a
smooth, natural polish.

Applications of a blended mixture of bees-wax and
American turpentine will heighten the natural colouring, accentuate the run of the grain, seal the pores
and help to protect the wood from extremes of tem-
perature and repeated handling. A matt or glossy
finish, as desired, will be produced depending on the
proportions of bees-wax and turpentine in the mixture.

Equipment for wax polishing

Medium-soft bristled brush, pan, quarter-filled with water, jar of blended bees-wax and American turpentine, clean soft duster.

16 The wax mixture is best applied warm. Heat over a low heat in a pan quarter-filled with water.

As the wax begins to melt, stir regularly until a

smooth warm liquid results. The preparation is now ready for use.

Hold the sculpture with the duster and apply the liquid wax mixture with the brush, thinly and evenly.

Starting at the top and quickly working downwards until the whole model is thinly coated.

When completed, leave to stand for twenty-four hours in warm, dust-free conditions.

17 As the wax soaks into the pores, it will tend to dry out leaving a dull looking coat which is then ready for polishing. A fairly stiff bristled hairbrush will be excellent for polishing and removing surplus wax.

18 Continue the brisk brushing and light polishing with
    a clean soft duster.
19 The finished sculpture, now with a light lustre wax
    polish and demonstrating stylised simple forms.

A partially integrated couple carving (laburnum). The natural features of the wood have been retained and incorporated in the carving as a whole.

Integrated couple (mother and child) carving (laburnum) making full use of natural features and run of grain.

Carving Single Figures in the Round

The first consideration in carving single figures will naturally be the carver's concept of imaginative idea of the image visualised as a whole. Whatever the subject, human forms, animals, birds, fish, reptiles, plant life, etc., it is first necessary to form a clear image in the mind of the subject viewed completely in the round. It should be harmoniously proportional from every aspect. The same principles employed in couple carving are applicable for carving single figures in the round.

Preliminary sketches and models may be of some help, but it is of the utmost importance to form a very clear visualisation of the finished sculpture as a whole. It is also of equal importance that the concept be compatible with the material to be used for the carving.

Once the idea has germinated, grown and formed, a piece of wood most suitable should be specifically selected. In some instances the basic idea often springs quite spontaneously when viewing or handling a particular piece of timber. When this occurs there is little difficulty. Often a carver may have a noble idea but may look a very long time for the timber best suited to execute the actual carving.

Always remember that the grain, colouring and texture of the wood will all play an important part in the final appearance of the sculpture.

If the idea happens to be of great importance, it may be advisable to select a timber where some of the more eccentric elements are lacking or greatly subdued. Lime and

Female standing figure
(oak).

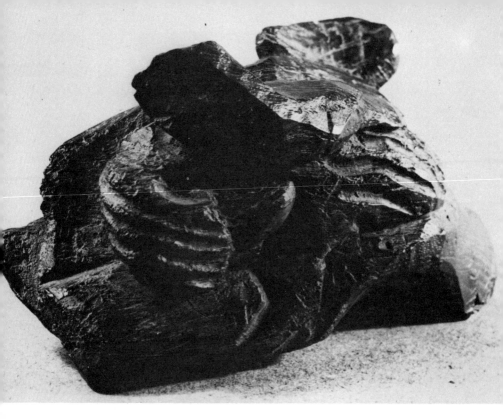

Fallen bird (11th-century oak).

Single figure (laburnum).

sycamore are usually selected for this type of working. They are also admirable carving timbers. Being easy working they are recommended for the beginner.

In order to avoid undue distraction, timbers with highly pronounced grain or exciting colouring need much consideration and marrying with the basic idea.

First and foremost, idea and image must be coupled with the most appropriate material for the execution of the model.

When carving a single figure, it should be borne in mind that there is essentially *one* focal point, i.e. the concept as a *whole*, with all the many minor details and highlights blended unobtrusively to accentuate the attitudes and relationship of forms and rhythms.

Reclining figure (laburnum).

Female torso (*English yew*).

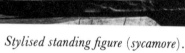

Stylised standing figure (sycamore).

Standing cloaked figure (rosewood).

Try to keep ideas simple and uncomplicated. The beginner has a tendency to forget or neglect the natural qualities inherent in the wood. The basic idea becomes over-dominant, especially in the minor details, and would be better executed in other media.

Make every effort to use and incorporate imaginatively the most manageable natural features of the wood.

Size and proportion play an important role, although a certain degree of exaggeration may lend significance to the piece. There are limits which should be estimated when initially selecting the material to be used.

Avoid undue expenditure of time and energy cutting away large areas of waste material. Aim for as little gouge cutting as possible by trying to visualise the model encased inside the block and taking up as much space as possible.

Cloaked figure (rosewood).

With little variations, the stages in carving follow the same pattern as that previously described for couple carving.

In all figure carving there are many tricky passages which require some ingenuity and inventive adaptation of tools. In general keep all chisels and gouges well sharpened. Carve with and across the grain wherever possible and take extra care when carving across the end-grain.

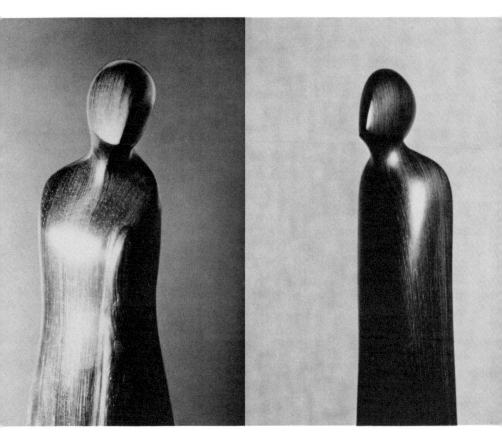

The effect of cutting across the end grain (rosewood).

Group Sculptures

The essence of any group sculpture is the impression created as a result of integrating three or more elements to form an expressive unity. The elements may consist of figures, animals, plants, architectural constructions, or indeed any subject which strengthens the total expression.

Group sculptures carved in wood are usually intended for indoor display or to be placed under some form of cover. Bronze or stone are usually employed for outdoor representations. When a group is intended to be displayed indoors, the size and proportions should be considered in relation to the surroundings and environment, e.g. public hall, church, house, etc.

Interesting groups, varying in complexity, can be carved from a single block of wood. Previous experience gained in carving single figures and couples will prove advantageous, together with a knowledge of the intricacies and exciting possibilities of single and multiple penetrations in relation to the natural form. Before starting, the relationship of the envisaged sculpture to the block of wood needs much careful thought and consideration.

Focal points of interest should be established and any distracting details which are not relevant should be eliminated. Aim for simplicity in the juxtaposition of the various forms and rhythms. State the main subject matter clearly and boldly, without losing sight of the natural elements embodied in the timber; these will play an important part and should be incorporated into the overall design. Pay particular attention to the run of the grain and its resulting appearance in the finished work.

Opposite: *The author refining a small group sculpture.*

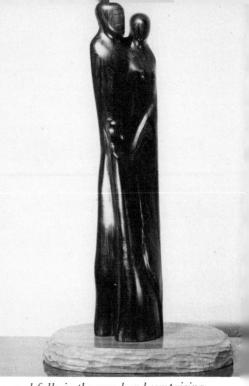

A unified rosewood family group carved fully in the round and comprising three figures making use of the natural features of the wood and run of grain; photographed from five different viewpoints.

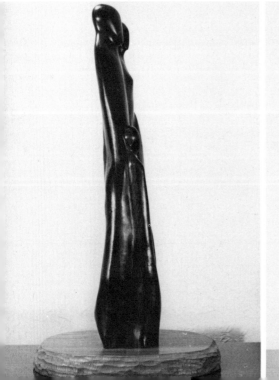

Viewpoint

Depending upon the intended display site for the sculpture, the carving of the group can be tackled in the following ways:

1 If the sculpture is to be placed in a niche or alcove, the bulk of the carving can be designed to be viewed entirely from the front, leaving little or no detailed forming at the back.
2 Where a model is to be placed against a wall, or tucked away in a corner, some continuation of the forms will need to be carried on round the returns.
3 A piece to be situated in a central position, where it can be viewed from almost any angle, will obviously need to be carved fully in the round.

The detailed working of the heads is shown in this close-up.

Whatever the method chosen, the effect of both natural and artificial light should be borne in mind. Both the subtle and the more dramatic effects of the play of light over the forms produce highlights and shadows which either detract or enhance the initial visual impact.

Group sculptures carved from a single block may have a marked degree of unification, be partially divided or linked in some way to join the various elements into an integrated whole. Group carving should be treated very much like music – with point, counter-point, harmonies, rhythms, etc. composed and fused to represent its own particular visual expression.

Opposite: *A stylised family group (rosewood) showing relative size and proportions. Notice the subtle expressive effect of highlight and shadow.*

Composite Sculptures

Composite groups consist of a number of sculptural elements which may be joined, partially linked or divided.

The traditional Christmas nativity crib is a good example of a composite sculpture group. There may be a great number of variations on this theme, but basically all are conveying the same message. Some are very elaborate, highly detailed and colourful, whilst others are of the utmost simplicity. Some cribs rely on ornate settings and impressive proportions, others stir the emotions through the expressive qualities and attitudes of the individual characters.

In a crib, the focal point of attention is obvious and all the other symbolic elements gravitate towards this point and guide the eye towards the centre.

A carver can learn a great deal by studying the work of great painters and sculptors, observing how all the elements are composed to form a harmonious whole. Through such study it becomes clear that the possibilities are limitless.

When considering carving a composite group for the first time, there is a tendency for the beginner to be over-ambitious.

In order to avoid disappointment, it is advisable to select themes which are well within one's grasp and the acquired technical carving ability. In our everyday lives we are always surrounded with suitable subjects, so there is no need to search far for sources of inspiration.

Choose simple, straightforward subjects and carve the statements strongly and directly, without any embellishment.

Opposite: *A composite group (alder and cherry) comprising three individual elements. The forms have been simplified and the group holds together by a visual linking of the relationship between the forms, rhythms and attitudes.*

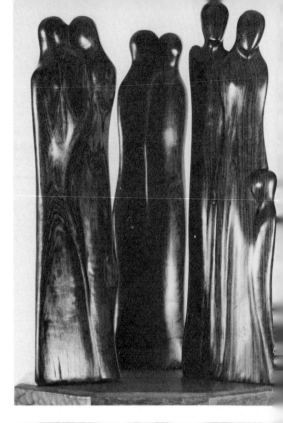

A composite group comprising three separate couple carvings, each couple carving being complete in itself. When placed in relationship with other elements, each couple contributes to a whole, resulting in an expressive composition. Being free standing, the individual pieces can be interchangeable, to form new and differing compositions.

Composite group of three interchangeable couple carvings. The effect of utilising the natural features of the timber (rosewood) is clearly illustrated. The individual couples have been re-arranged to form a new composition.

108

Summary Table
for Figure Carving

Category	Comprising	Attitudes, Gestures, Inclinations
Single figures	One figure	
Couple carvings	Involving two integrated figures	*Applicable to all Groups*
		Standing, sitting, kneeling, crouching, reclining
Groups	Three or more integrated figures	Stillness
Composites	Compositions of the above Groups. Unified, divided or both.	Suggestion of Movement Moods

Suppliers of Tools and Equipment

Suppliers
Alec Tiranti Ltd., 21 Goodge Place, London W1. 70 High Street, Theale, Berkshire.

Manufacturers
Henry Taylor (Acorn Brand), Woodside Works, Rutland Road, Sheffield.
W. Marples and Sons Ltd., Sheffield.

Further Reading

Carving Techniques Glynis Beecroft, Batsford, London
Sculpture in Wood P. Edward Norman, The Studio Publications, London
Wood Carving Alan Durst, How To Do It Series.
Woodcarving Charles Graveney, How To Do It Series.
Creative Wood Craft Ernst Rottger, Batsford, London.
Do It Yourself Natural Wood Sculpture John Matthews, Blandford Press, Poole.

Index